NOW LISTEN

NOW LISTEN

21 HABITS TO BETTER LISTEN TO YOURSELF, EACH OTHER, AND THE WORLD

AILEEN GIBB

Published by:
Aileen Gibb

"Learning how to listen and speak with each other are essential skills for creating relationships that lead to mutual respect, dialogue, understanding and peace. Listening encompasses much more than words. Listening is a way of being in the world."

–Kay Lindahl, The Sacred Art of Listening

Dedicated to all the listeners in my life...thank you.

CONTENTS

Foreword by Gary Diggins   11

Author's Introduction   15

A Definition of Listening   21

The 21 Habits   22

Opening   24

Section One - Listening to Self   32
   My Story: Part One   34
   Listening to Self   37
   Habits 1-7: Listening to Self 44
   Poem: "Questions" (Gary Diggins) 62

Section Two - Listening to Each Other   64

    My Story: Part Two   66

    Listening to Each Other   70

    Habits 8-14: Listening to Each Other   80

    Poem: "Listening" (Anonymous)   102

Section Three - Listening to the World   104

    My Story: Part Three   106

    Listening to the World   111

    Habits 15-21: Listening to the World   120

    Poem: "It's Time" (Aileen Gibb)   142

Closing   144

References and Resources   153

Additional References and Resources   157

Acknowledgements / Appreciations   159

About the Author   162

FOREWORD

By Gary Diggins

Past: Twenty years ago, I walked into a crowded Calgary café and scanned the room for someone I had never met before. Her name was Aileen Gibb. Once we connected and settled at a back table, I quickly realised that this woman was not only curious about the art of listening, but also passionate about applying this skill on multiple levels—as an individual practice, as a dynamic within organisational leadership, and as a catalytic agent in social change. We hit it off as kindred spirits. Immediately, Aileen invited me to contribute my musical abilities to a pilot course she was hosting on the Isle of Skye in Scotland.

Our subsequent collaborations over the years transported us to beautiful settings on the planet where we gathered with intimate or large groups of participants. The challenges facing each group would shift and change according to larger events or internal matters. One team might be facing a financial downturn in their industry. A year later, another configuration would be struggling to incorporate more diversity within their leadership group. Throughout all of these circumstantial fluctuations, Aileen's core work remained consistent. She persistently championed the value of human beings asking poignant questions, connecting authentically, and listening deeply.

Present: As I write this foreword, the outer circumstance of 2020's global pandemic has implicated us all. The gravity of this outbreak impacts our personal and professional lives: how people show up (or not) in the workplace, whether we travel (or not) for our vocations or vacations, and even whether we comply (or not) with safety protocols.

Amidst these months of uncertainty, Aileen is releasing a guidebook on the equally far-reaching effects of intentional listening. I would suggest that the timing is perfect! What better time to lean into the moment and apply these principles? How we listen to one another, to experts, and to our own inner guidance carries consequences into an interconnected web of people—from strangers, to our immediate circle of colleagues or loved ones, and everyone in between.

Future: True to her nature, Aileen's guidebook offers an array of inquisitive prompts that invite us to pause, ponder, and take action. Her business, Inspired Future, was predicated on helping individuals get clear on a goal or vision, and then take definitive steps to make a dream come true. She has embedded multi-faceted versions of listening into her coaching work. This book captures those practices, and wraps them up in an engaging way.

I imagine a reader rolling out of bed, brewing a coffee, taking in the rising sun, and picking up this book. Casually, the individual cracks open Aileen's publication to a random page. Suddenly, the person looks down and takes in these words:

"The more you practice listening to connect with each other, and hearing what each other care about, the more you learn about each other. One habit that's been revised during the 2020 lockdown is our casual greeting, 'How are you?' We've learned to get more curious and ask the deeper version of the question: 'How are you really today?' Try it with the next person you meet."

I feel another timely element in Aileen's book is that it acts as an invitation to slow down, drop down, and calm down. It's a chance to leave our frenetic and hectic cadences, and press pause on the need to scurry just to keep up with the exigencies of the day. In a more mindful state of being, we can accommodate Aileen's reflective content, including the inquiries and practices that enrich our relationship to self, other, and the world.

So, put on the coffee (or herbal tea). Look out the window to the larger world. Breathe in some solitude and quietude. Sit with an array of playful and meaningful nudges from each page. Take in Aileen's well-crafted anecdotes, quotes, and questions. Try out fresh ideas or timeless principles. Notice how your present awareness and future existence shift in subtle or dramatic ways.

An old Zen saying suggests that we are responsible for "looking the sky into blueness." Aileen's guidebook posits that we are invited to "listen the world into beauty and purpose."

–*Gary Diggins*
Author of *Tuning the Eardrum – Listening as a Mindful Practice.*

AUTHOR'S INTRODUCTION

"Listening is a radical act. You risk being changed by it."

–Juanita Brown, Founder of World Café

Tuesday, June 25, 2019, was when I heard the radical words that changed me:

"This," said my consultant, turning his computer screen toward my husband and me seated in front of his desk, "is your tumour."

Listening has been a core element in my work for more than 20 years. To some degree, it prepared me for that moment. I was surprised and curious. I didn't panic, or feel fear. I held my calm and listened as my consultant patiently explained what the MRI scan revealed.

It was a listening moment like no other I had experienced before, or that I have yet to experience again.

It brought home to me the fact that how we listen in any one moment shapes both our immediate response, and our subsequent relationship with whatever twists or turns our lives may take. What's more, it underscores that what we hear is at least a three-way collaboration between our inner knowing, the outer voices of others, and the guiding forces that shape us at specific points on our paths.

It would take me several more months to appreciate this collaboration, and to welcome it as the foundation for this book. While the idea of *Now Listen* had been brewing for some time, it wasn't until that June day that it fully came alive.

Listening is a recurring theme in my earlier books: *Asking Great Questions* and *The Conversation Edge*. A great question invites great listening, and they dance together in a great conversation. Such is the foundational importance of listening in leadership, and throughout the entirety of our lives, that I felt called to afford listening its own book—thereby completing what I hadn't anticipated would become a series of three companion texts. As with the earlier two books, my hope is that *Now Listen* will become your go-to for improving your daily listening.

I guess this book ought to be an audiobook, fulfilling its aim of inviting you to listen more deeply to yourself, to others, and to life around you as you explore tips and techniques that will hopefully resonate with you. I'll take that on board, and look forward to reading it aloud at some point. In the meantime, those of you who know me will likely hear the burr of my Scottish accent as you read it through. And, for those of you I have yet to meet, I hope you will hear your own voice echoing back from these pages as you slow down and reflect on the possibilities for greater listening amidst the noise of life.

It is indeed a noisy world out there. As I write this in early 2020, the majority of the world is in lockdown due to the coronavirus pandemic. In many ways, the world has gotten even noisier with so much of life moving online. I realise I've moved far from that sacred listening moment in my consultant's office, as I find myself endlessly scrolling on social media, and listening to televised broadcasts and political podcasts from the UK and Canada (as a dual citizen, I'm absorbed by how the story is unfolding on both sides of the Atlantic).

As some people speed up and others slow down, I hear the need for listening come more sharply into focus. I'm coaching constantly on the importance of listening IN to hear what we haven't heard before as we move through this experience together. I'm curious what we will hear on the other side of it.

I wasn't intending for this book to be specifically about a pandemic situation, and it's likely (I hope) that the immediate stress of the pandemic might be over by the time it is published. At the same time, I can't ignore the current context. I had thought to shape *Now Listen* around my own story as it unfolded from the moment I learned about my tumour. I wouldn't be surprised to find that the greater story of our time—a virus that spreads to all corners of our globe, and connects people from all nations in a way we're only now waking up to—will also guide these pages.

My focus is on BEING a listener, whilst I also direct you to other books and resources to help you DO listening.

Listening is a lifelong practice for most of us. People usually tell me they're quite good at listening, unaware they are sabotaging their own listening by constantly checking email or mobile phone messages, talking over each other, or rushing through conversations, then acting on assumptions and half-baked information.

This book invites you to slow down, pay attention, and develop new listening habits.

You can pick this book up at any point in your day and flick it open to find something useful. You can read some of the content pieces, and see what jumps out at you. Or, you can turn to the "7 habits" pages, and choose one habit to focus on at a time. If you choose one habit daily, you'd be practicing 21 habits over 21 days (roughly an average working month).

For another approach, you can pick one habit and practice it for an entire week or month, in order to enrich and sustain your listening experience over time.

If in some small way this book inspires your enhanced listening to go viral as a force for learning and change, then I'll consider it my small contribution to an emerging new world.

I invite you now to press pause and listen for what these pages want you to hear.

Yes, it might change you.

Indeed, I hope it changes us all to some degree...and to some good.

—Aileen

A DEFINITION OF LISTENING

I didn't know there was a Global Listening Centre. I found it at https://www.globallisteningcentre.org.

They define listening as:

> "a global, multimodal process that underlies effective interpersonal and intercultural relations. Listening is part attitude, marked by genuine respect and regard for all; part skill, enabled by specific verbal and nonverbal behaviors; and part physical, driven by a host of physiological, sensory-motor, cognitive, and affective functions. Combined, these elements shape the perceptual lenses through which humans interpret and strive to understand themselves, colored by each individual's cultural background." [1]

Their hope is not to set 'the' definition for all to follow, but instead to propose a broad, inclusive way in which we can all view and understand what listening is.

THE 21 HABITS

HABITS 1 – 7: LISTENING TO SELF

1. First, Listen to Yourself
2. Listen with Head and Heart
3. Healthy Body, Healthy Mind, Healthy Listening
4. Learn to W.A.I.T.
5. Good Self-talk
6. Ask for Feedback
7. Your Daily Reflective Listening Ritual

HABITS 8 – 14: LISTENING TO EACH OTHER

8. Be P.U.R.E. in Your Listening Intention
9. Listen to Connect
10. Care About What's Important
11. Be Curious to Hear What You Don't Know
12. S.T.O.P. Talking (So the Other Person Can Talk)
13. Agreement and Completion
14. Enjoy the Silence

HABITS 15 – 21: LISTENING TO THE WORLD

15.   Listen for New Perspectives

16.   Listen with Head, Heart and Hand

17.   We ARE All Connected

18.   Practice Radical Curiosity

19.   Blue Sky Listening

20.   Leave a Legacy of Listening

21.   Create Listening Circles

OPENING

"For a word to be spoken, there must be silence.
Before and after."

–Ursula K. Le Guin, from A Wizard of Earthsea

When I catch a quiet day on my favourite ski run, I stop halfway down and listen to the deep silence of the mountain.

Well, I used to.

Tinnitus means that I will never truly know silence again. My world is tainted by a persistent ringing on the left side of my skull. My life plays out daily to the never-ending echo of a lightly struck tuning fork, resonating constantly despite the fact that I am now totally deaf in my left ear.

My work depends on deep listening, and here I am putting my insights into a book about that very topic. Rather than being a limitation, I've found that my tinnitus and one-eared deafness actually enhance my listening.

My tinnitus disappears into the background when I'm talking, or when I'm listening intently to another person. It serves as a form of white noise; all other interference fades into the background. I simply don't notice it.

One client generously remarked that even with one functioning eardrum, I still listen better than most people do with two. I'd claim that this skill comes from years of conscious practice. With that said, one intention for this book is that it inspires and supports you to also commit to honing your innate listening skills. That way, to echo the Ursula K. Le Guin quote above, every word can receive silent space in which to be heard.

To me, this quote infers that being spoken also means being heard. Is a word truly spoken if it doesn't land on a receptive ear and become meaningful to the receiver? Is it otherwise nothing more than another contribution to the cacophony of sound we struggle to listen through every moment of every day? Indeed, every word *deserves* silent space from where it can be held and heard.

Our world is fast and noisy. In his book, *Volume Control*, David Owen describes the increasing incidence of deafness in the population.[2] It is a condition that most people neglect for up to 10 years, assuming it to be a natural part of the aging process. Turning up the TV and shouting to be heard are not solutions. Once your hearing is compromised, as I now know, it doesn't come back.

Over time, listening may diminish on physical, mental, and emotional levels, which can affect many aspects of our lives and relationships. We owe it to ourselves to more consciously develop, strengthen, and enhance our listening skills, and to create healthier listening environments.

As in my earlier books, I invite you to approach listening at this level as a life practice. There are many books on improving your listening skills. Interestingly enough, the past few years have seen an explosion in books alluding to our increased need for more silence in a noisy world. ("Silence in a Noisy World" had actually been the working subtitle for *Now Listen*, until I discovered how many other books had beaten me to that title!)

Like any skill, listening invites conscious and applied practice. Similar to honing any other muscle and aptitude, listening improves as you give it more attention.

I imagine that you're considering this book because, on some level, you know you're not quite as good a listener as you sometimes pretend to be. If you're like most people (including myself, despite decades of conscious practice) you turn your listening on and off in different contexts and with different people.

You've likely developed habits of listening and non-listening that others notice before you recognise them in yourself. And, you're likely using significant energy to combat the inefficiency of poor listening—repeating yourself, revisiting conversations, and wasting time with misunderstandings and assumptions.

There's nothing new in this book that likely hasn't been suggested elsewhere. So, if this book is to make a difference for you, your work, your relationships, and your life, it will need to be something you're willing to pick up regularly and experiment with.

I don't anticipate that you'll read it from front to back. It doesn't matter where you start. What does matter is that you bring with you an intention to hear something that jumps off a page and resonates; that you consider one or more of the 21 habits that follow worth introducing into your life; and, that you hear the possibilities this book contains.

A popular piece of Jewish folklore alludes to how the black ink of the words on a page immediately grab our focus when we open a book. We tend to only see the ink, because we're habituated to expecting a story to read, or information to assimilate. Yet, a whole field of whitespace exists behind and around the words—without which, the words would not be supported or formatted. Indeed, the white space holds the story to be read.

We have a similar experience in our listening. We hear what we *want* to hear, what we *expect* to hear, and what we *assume* we will hear. All too often, our listening stays at that superficial level, even though this can leave us unfulfilled, confused, or no more informed that when we started a conversation or meeting.

Like the white page behind words, there's a big world of silence to explore beyond the words and superficial noise of chitchat, throwaway comments, questions to which we don't wait for answers, the constant drone of TV or radio, our addictions to screens and mobile devices, and even our growing dependencies on the likes of Alexa and Siri.

It takes layers of listening to open up that vast silence. When we learn to listen more deeply into that silence, we discover so much more about ourselves, about each other, and about our world.

This book invites you to do so across three sections, each one containing seven suggested listening habits:

- **Section One** is about listening to yourself, your inner voice, your thoughts and your intuitions.

- **Section Two** looks at listening to each other—where, quite possibly, our greatest challenges, and our greatest potential gifts lie.

- **Section Three** goes into listening to the world. Like whitespace on a page, listening to the world holds you in every moment and experience, and gives context to how life unfolds.

The first habit in each section delves into the intention you bring to listening, while each section's last habit offers a suggested listening ritual.

If you have read my earlier book, *The Conversation Edge*, you'll 'get' that the other five habits within each section follow the five 'C's of conversation:

- Connecting
- Caring
- Curiosity
- Clarity
- Completion

Don't worry—my previous book is not a prerequisite for *Now Listen,* and these stages equally apply to the way we bring listening into conversations.

Could each section offer more than seven habits? Of course. Some listening books are hundreds of pages long, and go into the psychological, physical and philosophical layers of listening.

For me, I want this book to do its work on *your* listening—and for you to help it along the way. Therefore, on the page opposite each habit, you'll find space for journaling and notes, so you can actively work on the suggested habit, take time to reflect, and uncover how to work with the habit in your life.

Your journal pages can be places you revisit often, whether to review your notes, or add new ones related to your listening experience. You can also use the journal space to create an ongoing record of how you develop as a listener, and to note things that shift and change for you and your listening over time.

I hope that the practical design will make *Now Listen* an easy and useful tool you can reach for every day, flick open to a page, and discover an immediate idea or insight that will positively affect the way you listen and hear.

SECTION ONE

LISTENING TO SELF

"Listen to the wind - it talks.
Listen to the silence - it speaks.
Listen to your heart - it knows."

–Native American Proverb

MY STORY

Part One

One morning in February, 2019, I woke up with a nauseous head-ache. It wasn't debilitating. I could easily have turned over and slept it off. Yet something urged me to pay attention.

Lately, I'd put my headaches down to sinus problems, having recently returned to the damp Scottish air. However, this seemed different. I heard my mother's voice. A retired nursing sister, she always said that headaches plus nausea could be serious, and ought not to be ignored.

It was already midmorning when I picked up the phone to call the doctor. As expected, there were no more appointments that day. I was offered a time three weeks down the road. I remember pausing for a long moment of silence before I spoke. Very slowly and gently, I heard myself say:

"I might not be here in three weeks' time."

I was only half joking.

I was confident that this was not a case of normal flu. The receptionist, trained to listen deeply for sometimes over-neurotic patients, eventually heard me. She gave me an emergency appointment, warning me that I'd have to wait till whenever a doctor became free. I was relieved. I'd been heard.

By two o'clock that same afternoon, I'd had a thorough checkup. My doctor couldn't find an obvious cause for my headache. I expected her to say there was nothing much wrong, and to come back if it happened again.

It would not have been unreasonable to expect her to send me home with some pain medication. Instead, she'd listened deeply enough to join the dots as I explained symptoms beyond the headache, and refer me for a specialist ENT consultation.

I remember that long moment when I sat on the sofa with the phone in my hand. How I held on to that moment. How I listened

IN to the silence, and how the receptionist waited for me to speak again. How I knew that I had to ask for what I needed.

It would have been easy to let any of the other voices scrambling for space in my head take over:

"It's nothing serious."
"You're being dramatic."
"It's only a headache."
"You're wasting the doctor's time."
"It'll go away on its own."

Or, perhaps to ignore the one that was also saying:

"What if this is serious?"

It wasn't until I slowed down and listened to the many layers of voices running through my head, that I finally and clearly heard the one voice, deep inside, that called me to act—the one I nearly missed.

LISTENING TO SELF

"Have you ever listened to people from the inside?
Listened so close you can hear their thoughts—and
all their memories. Hear them think from places they
don't even known they think from?"

–From the movie Powder

This may be one of my favourite quotes of all time. I've used it in all three of my books. I hear it now as an invitation to listen inside myself—to realise there's a place I can listen from that's very powerful, yet all too often not fully heard.

It's beyond listening just with my ears.

Percussionist Evelyn Glennie, who hails from a small village in North East Scotland just five miles from my own home village— and who therefore has a soft rolling accent similar to my own—is on a mission to teach the world to listen more deeply. She invites us to listen with the entirety of our bodies.

Evelyn learned that listening extends beyond the ears when her hearing started to fail at age 11. She didn't let that stop her. In fact, it led her to question how else she could listen, and spurred her on to pursue new methods of hearing. In her 2007 TED talk, "How to Truly Listen," she shows us how to bring listening alive. It is really quite inspiring.[3]

The first time I heard my friend, sound practitioner Gary Diggins, demonstrate throat singing, I realised how I could hear with more than my ears. We were in a white stone chapel at a sanctuary near Austin, Texas. We'd gone in to admire the building's simplicity and beauty. Suddenly, Gary started to sing. His voice sounded like an entire orchestra playing all at once. I could hear at least half a dozen different tones coming from Gary's voice. I was speechless, and in tears. In that magical moment, I opened up to the latent potential of the human voice, and our innate capacity to hear much more than the surface layers our ears are trained to receive.

What, I asked, had I been missing in all my years of listening, if I hadn't been using the full extent of my listening range?

Learning to listen with more of my senses, I often wonder:

"What am I seeing, hearing, feeling, thinking, sensing, experiencing, missing, fearing, or enjoying in this moment?"

I still ask myself this question when facilitating groups, coaching one to one, and even when I'm with family or friends. It brings me to a deeper layer of awareness, and helps me hear what's going on inside me, before I respond to others.

I'm listening to *how* I'm listening.

Can you distinguish what you're hearing inside yourself from what you're hearing in the world outside you?

Do you find it easier to listen to the world outside you than to listen deeply inside yourself? One of my fellow coaches revealed the following in a recent conversation:

"I listen to other people, so I don't have to listen to myself."

When you listen more deeply to yourself, you might find:

- You get really uncomfortable, because you're touching something that you haven't wanted to hear or explore, and which your mind has told you isn't going to be easy.
- You discover that when you listen more closely, what you hear is helpful, freeing, and empowering—perhaps even exactly what you need at that moment.
- You realise that you hear a story that has been holding you back. In the end, you may even laugh at how easily you shift gears and free yourself from it.

A coaching conversation is an opportunity to stop and listen to yourself more deeply. As I say to clients, coaching creates a space where you get an extra:

- Pair of ears to listen to yourself.
- Set of eyes to look at your life.
- Voice to ask questions you don't ask yourself.
- Heart that opens up to your true feelings, perceptions and possibilities.
- Pair of hands to nudge you into action when needed.

Many of my clients say a coaching conversation is one they don't get anywhere else—where they can hear themselves think, and listen to their inner voice.

So, what do you discover when you listen more deeply to yourself? It's where more of your potential exists. It's an invitation to a journey of self-awareness and self-discovery.

Like the coaching colleague I mentioned above, you might be cautious to open the door to your innermost thoughts, feelings, and ideas. After all, you don't know where they will take you.

Yet, that's the adventure, isn't it? You *don't know* where you'll go. If you don't listen to your own yellow brick road, you may never discover what's waiting for you. No matter what stage of life you're at, there's likely more to hear when you consciously listen IN to all of your layers.

Self-listening is a way to slow down, become more aware, choose your responses more consciously, and show up more fully. It's a pathway to self-learning and personal growth.

As Evelyn Glennie and Gary Diggins show us, we can listen with all of our senses and emotions to create beautiful music within ourselves—and from which we can bring more of our voices into the world.

In his book, *Beauty: The Invisible Embrace*, John O'Donohue, an Irish poet and philosopher—and a personal source of inspiration—calls it the "voice of your own soul."

As he writes:

"When you take time to draw on your listening imagination, you will begin to hear this gentle voice at the heart of your life. It is deeper and surer than all the other voices of disappointment, unease, self-criticism and bleakness. It's always there and the more deeply you learn to listen, the greater surprises and discoveries that will unfold." [4]

The poet, Mark Nepo, has a book entitled *Seven Thousand Ways to Listen: Staying Close to What is Sacred*. [5] It's a lovely book of reflective questions that invite deep self-listening. Seven thousand ways sounds a bit overwhelming, yet it does perhaps highlight the complexity and depth of what it means to really listen. If only it could be simple!

As for choosing just *seven* listening habits to start, my efforts turned out to be trickier than I first thought they would.

Whenever I picked something that seemed like a useful listening habit, I could not clarify whether it was a habit for listening to yourself, or for listening to others. I concluded that most aspects of listening involve both. In the end, listening as a practice of its own requires that we ask the following:

"Am I listening to myself, or truly listening to the other person?"

Even this one question will shift your listening to a new level.

HABITS 1–7

LISTENING TO SELF

1. First, Listen to Yourself
2. Listen with Head and Heart
3. Healthy Body, Healthy Mind, Healthy Listening
4. Learn to W.A.I.T.
5. Good Self-talk
6. Ask for Feedback
7. Your Daily Reflective Listening Ritual

HABIT 1

FIRST, LISTEN TO YOURSELF

Set your intention daily to listen more attentively to yourself. I suggest this might invite you to slow down and pause more often amid your busy-ness. One of the habits of many successful people is to start the day with an intention. What if your daily intention is to listen to yourself first, and to hear your own needs, wants, and desires before you give yourself over to what others ask of you?

Develop the habit of intentionally listening and asking questions of yourself:

- What's going on in my head and my heart?
- What am I ready to listen for?
- What's distracting or rushing me?
- What do I hear in myself when I slow down?

How, where, when, with whom, might you apply this habit in your work and life?

Practice this habit for one full day. What do you notice and learn?

After one week of using this habit in your life and work, what is different?

Return to this habit after one month. How has it impacted you, your conversations, your relationships, your leadership, your work, and your life? How do you now rate yourself as a listener?

HABIT 2
LISTEN WITH HEAD AND HEART

Real integrity is self-integrity, which means keeping your word and your promises to YOURSELF. The practice here is to know that you are the only person who hears yourself fully. Can you hear those sneaky little white lies and excuses you make to yourself? Can you quieten them, and be in full integrity with your own heart?

Ask yourself:

- How well do I stay true to my own heart?
- How well do I listen to the promises I make to myself?
- How do I feel when I hold to this level of self-truth?

How, where, when, with whom, might you apply this habit in your work and life?

Practice this habit for one full day. What do you notice and learn?

After one week of using this habit in your life and work, what is different?

Return to this habit after one month. How has it impacted you, your conversations, your relationships, your leadership, your work, and your life? How do you now rate yourself as a listener?

HABIT 3

HEALTHY BODY, HEALTHY MIND, HEALTHY LISTENING

Feelings of exhaustion, overwhelm, burnout, impatience, and frustration all lead to diminished listening. The noise becomes too much, and you can't hear yourself. With this in mind, what daily rituals do you follow in order to be the best version of your listening self?

When you bring your attention to your breath, notice that if you exhale slowly, and for longer than your inhale—perhaps twice as long—you can feel your body relax, and your attention sink down into your belly and legs. That's a great state from where to listen.

Now, ask yourself:

• What do I hear when I listen deeply to my body, heart and mind?

How, where, when, with whom, might you apply this habit in your work and life?

Practice this habit for one full day. What do you notice and learn?

After one week of using this habit in your life and work, what is different?

Return to this habit after one month. How has it impacted you, your conversations, your relationships, your leadership, your work, and your life? How do you now rate yourself as a listener?

HABIT 4

LEARN TO W.A.I.T (WHY AM I TALKING?)

Do you really hear yourself when you are talking? Just today, I saw a post from Bernard Looney, chief executive at the global corporation, BP plc, where he reminds us of one of his mother's favorite sayings: We have two ears and one mouth, and should use them in that proportion.[6]

I've seen and heard lots of people mentioning this phrase lately, yet it seems hard to live up to. The habit here is to first hear yourself, and then realise that you may be talking too much.

Make it a habit to **W.A.I.T.**, and ask:

- **W**hy **A**m **I T**alking?
- With this awareness, move into listening.

How, where, when, with whom, might you apply this habit in your work and life?

Practice this habit for one full day. What do you notice and learn?

After one week of using this habit in your life and work, what is different?

Return to this habit after one month. How has it impacted you, your conversations, your relationships, your leadership, your work, and your life? How do you now rate yourself as a listener?

HABIT 5
GOOD SELF-TALK

What do you hear when you talk about yourself? Is it positive and uplifting? Or, do your verbal habits include words such as *sorry, should, just, perhaps, maybe,* or *but*? Do you use *we* or *you* when you really mean *I*? Are you always making excuses? This is known in the coaching world as Inner Game Interference—it gets in the way, and requires that you turn down the volume to clear the way to your best self. Hearing, then removing these habituated words, will change the way you show up in the world. Talking well about yourself isn't bragging, or being selfish. Instead, it's hearing who you are, and acknowledging what you contribute.

My client, Sheila, was planning her week, seeking to balance her business goals with being a mother. "I'll work Monday to Thursday," she said, "then take Friday off with the kids...unless a client needs to meet with me." I repeated her words back, then asked, "What if you shift from 'off' to 'on' with the kids?" She lit up with a smile. Her full commitment to family was evident instantaneously. No client would get to squeeze into her Fridays now. One small, two-letter word, made a huge difference to hearing herself.

What small word habits might shift everything for you?

How, where, when, with whom, might you apply this habit in your work and life?

Practice this habit for one full day. What do you notice and learn?

After one week of using this habit in your life and work, what is different?

Return to this habit after one month. How has it impacted you, your conversations, your relationships, your leadership, your work, and your life? How do you now rate yourself as a listener?

HABIT 6

ASK FOR FEEDBACK

Learn to listen beyond what you already know of yourself. Each day, ask someone for a suggestion on one thing they admire about you. It may sound selfish, but really, how else will you truly hear how people experience you? It's called *learning feedback*. Personally, I don't like the word 'feedback'. It's fraught with fears of criticism and judgement, and can prevent you from receiving useful insights. Guru coach Marshall Goldsmith prefers that we ask for *feed-forward*.[7] To do so:

- Be open to telling people that you're working on your listening skills.
- Then, ask them to suggest something you can focus on to be a better listener.
- Consider a question such as, "What's one aspect of listening I might improve?"

Most importantly, receive their insights with curiosity, and listen inside yourself to hear how it lands as a truth. From that place of awareness, you can work on things if you choose.

Hearing other perspectives is only one piece of data, and you are free to decide how to use or apply it. You may find that people who know you best are the most useful sources of insight as you consider your self-awareness and learning.

How, where, when, with whom, might you apply this habit in your work and life?

Practice this habit for one full day. What do you notice and learn?

After one week of using this habit in your life and work, what is different?

Return to this habit after one month. How has it impacted you, your conversations, your relationships, your leadership, your work, and your life? How do you now rate yourself as a listener?

HABIT 7

YOUR DAILY REFLECTIVE LISTENING RITUAL

Many self-help books recommend an end-of-day gratitude ritual, where you take time to reflect on three things you're thankful for from your day. I suggest extending this idea to an appreciation ritual.

Each day, reflect on:

- What are three things I appreciate about myself?
- How did my listening serve me well today?
- Where was my listening not quite as good as I intended today?

In keeping with the theme and intention of this book, I invite you to keep notes on your daily listening. Don't worry if your listening needs more work. Acknowledging places where you need to grow will bring new opportunities into your awareness.

You may even decide to return to Habit 1, and set an intention to practice tomorrow.

How, where, when, with whom, might you apply this habit in your work and life?

....

....

....

Practice this habit for one full day. What do you notice and learn?

....

....

....

After one week of using this habit in your life and work, what is different?

....

....

....

Return to this habit after one month. How has it impacted you, your conversations, your relationships, your leadership, your work, and your life? How do you now rate yourself as a listener?

....

....

....

....

QUESTIONS

I have sat on hard chairs
listening to informed speakers
delivering rigorous research

I have sat on soft cushions
listening to inspired teachers
delivering deep dharma talks

This afternoon
I can't recall any scientific statistics
or what Krishna said to Arjuna

I do remember Aileen's probing questions
sprinkled along our treks in Scottish landscapes

Where are you staying small?
What dream is pursuing you?
What are you willing to risk?

The telling and teaching of sages has its place

Still

my little vessel has been largely navigated
by the small rudder of tenacious questions
by the full sail of spacious conversations

In the end
questions are freely given

advice is getting pretty pricey these days[8]

–Gary Diggins

SECTION TWO

LISTENING TO EACH OTHER

"True listening is another way of bringing stillness into the relationship. When you truly listen to someone, the dimension of stillness arises and becomes an essential part of the relationship."

–Eckhart Tolle, from Stillness Speaks

MY STORY

Part Two

Three weeks after my doctor referred me, I met Mr. Frost, a ready-for-retirement ENT consultant. Mr. Frost would listen to several signals at the same time. He told me about a skiing trip that landed him in the hospital, whilst all the time working out how to tell me what he'd found in my test results.

I heard his exact words:

"Small nodules sometimes grow on the auditory nerves. In the 'olden times' they used to drill into your head to cut them out."

We laughed at that last bit. I didn't listen any deeper to ask him more questions. At this stage, I wasn't concerned, even when he said the next step was to refer me for an MRI scan. I was hearing what I wanted to hear. Action was being taken. I wasn't listening beyond the practical next steps.

My listening changed when those next steps accelerated into bigger strides.

Within four days of my scan, we were at a first meeting with new consultants, Mr. Ram and Mr. Kamel. A nurse, and a speech therapist, were also in the room. I was impressed. So many experts. I must be in good hands.

Still unconcerned, and studying the situation through the lens of my biases, I quickly noticed the listening skills that the two consultants demonstrated. They asked questions about my symptoms, listened attentively, and caught each other's nods as my symptoms stacked up and confirmed their suspicions.

Yes, my balance was a bit off. Yes, I was losing hearing in my left ear. Yes, I'd had an episode of vertigo. No, I couldn't walk in a straight line, heel to toe, without looking a bit tipsy. No, my left index finger did not immediately land on the tip of my nose when I swung my arm from an outstretched position as they asked me to. I missed my nose by about two inches. It all seemed a bit funny.

Just as it dawned on me that something more significant was happening, Mr. Kamel turned his computer screen toward me, and used the 'T' word:

"...and this is your tumour..."

I think I laughed, perhaps with surprise, possibly with denial, and certainly in disbelief.

"What do you mean, 'tumour'?"

I listened again. The big words; the little details; the prognosis; the treatment plan. I felt I was listening to a hospital drama on TV, except now I had the starring role in the series finale cliff hanger.

Even as I signed the consent form, I was still not sure what I'd heard.

"Come back on Friday," they said. "Ask us anything."

Impressed with their focused listening and genuine concern for my case, I was grateful that they were prepared to give me more of their precious time.

Driving home, I needed to hear myself say it all aloud:

"Twelve to eighteen hours in surgery.
Intensive care unit.
High-dependency ward.
Seven days in the hospital.
Five facial nerves.
Four titanium screws.
Three MRIs.
Two CAT scans.
One-sided hearing loss.
And drugs: anesthetics, steroids, antibiotics, pain blockers."

Even as I heard the information rolling out of my own mouth, I kept thinking about how brilliant my consultants were at listening. Maybe I was being willfully deaf to my situation. I wanted to understand how these skilled surgeons, who would carry out this highly complicated surgery, had such an amazing capacity for compassion, connection, and caring. What they showed was what I call human-level listening. It laid an amazing foundation for trust, and, no doubt, was the reason why I felt no fear putting my life in their hands.

LISTENING TO EACH OTHER

"The most basic and powerful way to connect to another person is to listen. Just listen. Perhaps the most important thing we ever give each other is our attention...A loving silence often has far more power to heal and to connect than the most well-intentioned words."

–Rachel Naomi Remen

Doctors have limited time to see patients. On average, they make a diagnosis after listening to a patient for only 29 seconds. What's more, recent studies indicate that they listen for only 11 seconds before they interrupt patients.[9]

What would happen if they could spare even just 10 more seconds to listen? Chances are, they would make different diagnoses, and prescribe more-effective drugs and treatment options.

It's not just doctors who jump too quickly to conclusions, or who think faster than the other person can speak. And, it's not only medical patients who go without being heard fully, sent off with solutions that don't match their needs.

Every day, in all facets of life, time, money, and energy are wasted, and people walk away with wrong solutions because someone else either misinterpreted, or didn't listen to their problem completely.

Listening is an untapped superpower. Unleashing it for an extra 10 seconds lets us hear more of each other, and can make huge, life-saving differences.

What are you really hearing when you listen to another person? Often, what you hear are your own thoughts *interpreting* what you think the other person is saying. Many leaders (parents, spouses, and friends too) think listening to another person is about working them out. The thought goes like this:

"If I can 'work out' this other person, then I'll know how to lead, manage, influence, or even control them."

Yet, to quote Miles Davis, the great jazz musician:

"If you understood everything I said, you'd be me."

Listening takes on new, deeper dimensions when you recognise that you can never fully understand another person. As soon as you think you already understand someone, or you've made up your mind about them, there's a good chance that you stop fully listening to them.

Contrary to even the listening experts who urge 'empathic listening', the words of former Archbishop of Canterbury, Rowan Williams, give me pause:

"Real empathy," he says, "is when we accept that we can *never* fully understand another person's experience."

Everyone's experience belongs solely to them. You can only listen with appreciation as they seek to explain and explore something. That's the beauty of the listening space—you can hear how another person's words relate to your own experience and perspectives.

Sometimes, they come together.

Sometimes, you learn from each other.

Sometimes, you're changed by listening to each other.

And sometimes, none of these things happen.

Real listening is a lifelong commitment. It creates a space where different perspectives, experiences, and needs can dance together. I'm sure you have noticed times when this ideal result doesn't occur. Lack of listening leads people to push each other apart, disagree, or fight.

What is it you are listening for? To confirm something you already think, or have decided? To provide answers? Fix a problem? To make someone feel better?

Or, are you listening for something you don't already know? To learn something about the other person's experience? To ask questions? To inspire new exploration or possibilities? Are you listening to the meaning behind the words? Can you hear what's not being spoken?

Some experts suggest we can't hear something in another person if we don't hear it first in ourselves. Yet, I find that listening to someone else also helps me hear things in myself.

When I'm listening to clients in coaching conversations, I give them all of my focus. When I am relaxing after a client conversation, I often get a big *Aha,* and realise the conversation offered me something I needed to hear. I gain a post-coaching insight, or a question that is relevant to my own life.

I've learned never to underestimate the power of the listening space as a mutual experience. It's an insightful exchange when we participate fully in it.

In his lovely book, *Conversation: How Talk Can Change Our Lives,* Theodore Zeldin invites us to:

"Enter into a conversation, willing to be changed by it."

This doesn't mean giving up your own ideas, or just letting someone else be 'right'. Nor does it mean that by listening you are agreeing with the other person. It does mean, however, that you allow your ideas to sit alongside those of others, willing to hear what's beyond your current thinking or assumptions. It means openly listening to the layers underneath the surface in order to learn, grow, and find new solutions and possibilities.

One of the great gifts of my work as a coach is that I get to listen to these layers in another person. Coaching works because it fundamentally relies on a deeper level of listening. The intention behind coaching is to be changed and moved to action by what emerges in the conversation. Just as Zeldin writes, it is this change that transforms lives—and it starts with listening.

Now, I invite you to be the listening professional when you are with another person. We find ourselves at a time in history when organisational leaders are called upon to be more coach-like than ever. For them—and for you, I presume—this means being willing to listen in entirely new ways. It also means accepting that it is impossible, and unnecessary, for any one person to hold all of the answers.

One of the most inspiring ways to invite contribution from everyone in your organisation is to listen to every idea and possibility that people offer.

True listening takes us below the surface. In that way, it's similar to the oft-used iceberg analogy—there's more to it than we know, or can readily observe. We must dive underneath our assumptions and judgements, and get to where real human treasure can be unearthed. That way, we can hear the hidden jewels we each carry, give them the polish they deserve, and bring them into the light.

In a 2019 blog post, Joost Minnaar of Corporate Rebels suggests that senior leaders see or hear only 4% of the real challenges and problems in their organisations.[10] Listening to their managers would reveal another 9%, while listening to their team leads will reveal up to 74%.

Meanwhile, the people who see almost 100% of real problems are working on the ground. Listening to them is vital.

In the mid 1990s, my mother was a senior nursing sister, nearing retirement. Around that time, the UK National Health Service introduced business managers 'to run hospitals more efficiently'.

Not one business manager asked my mother, with her 40 years of experience, how to improve her ward. Instead, they imposed changes, based on decisions made in some office or conference room. The changes adversely affected my mother's job satisfaction, frustrated her with more paperwork, and interfered with the true patient care to which she and her team were devoted.

Where might our health services be today if the dedicated wisdom of nurses had been heard all those years ago? In the spotlight of the 2020 pandemic, I hear a new generation of nurses feeling similarly un-consulted and unheard on issues that involve them as first-line responders.

If Joost Minnaar's statistics are any indication, the 'leaders' may still be making decisions based on less that 10% of what's actually happening. I can't help but wonder what they're missing by not listening better.

Margaret Heffernan has a fascinating book entitled *Willful Blindness*, and a TED Talk on the same topic.[11] We might as easily refer to the above health services example as *willful deafness*. Our ears can't help hearing things, yet our minds remain sneakily complicit in helping us shut out the things we don't want to hear.

"Can you hear me?"
"Are you listening?"
"What did you say?"
"Would you repeat that please?"
"Why didn't you ask me?"
"Why didn't you say so?"

Each familiar refrain exists in a world where distracted listening and willful deafness prevail. With our always-on devices, we display increasing levels of anxiety about missing a text or a phone call, yet remain willfully deaf to what the people nearby want us to hear.

There's plenty of room for practice, wouldn't you say?

HABITS 8 – 14

LISTENING TO EACH OTHER

8. Be P.U.R.E in Your Listening Intention

9. Listen to Connect

10. Care About What's Important

11. Be Curious to Hear What You Don't Know

12. S.T.O.P. Talking (So the Other Person Can Talk)

13. Agreement and Completion

14. Enjoy the Silence

HABIT 8

BE P.U.R.E IN YOUR LISTENING INTENTION

My guess is that you spend much less time preparing to listen to others than you do preparing to talk at your next presentation. The P.U.R.E. intention is how a great coach creates the space for another person to be fully heard.

You can bring the same intention to all conversations and relationships with the **P.U.R.E.** habit by being:

- **P**resent, with nothing distracting you;
- **U**nattached to any predetermined or imagined outcome;
- **R**eady to focus your attention on the person and conversation; and
- **E**ngaged fully in what is about to unfold.

How, where, when, with whom, might you apply this habit in your work and life?

....

....

....

....

Practice this habit for one full day. What do you notice and learn?

....

....

....

....

After one week of using this habit in your life and work, what is different?

....

....

....

....

Return to this habit after one month. How has it impacted you, your conversations, your relationships, your leadership, your work, and your life? How do you now rate yourself as a listener?

....

....

....

....

....

HABIT 9
LISTEN TO CONNECT

"Does the space between us connect us, or push us apart?"

This question, which I came upon years ago, stays with me. Being trained to have a 'right' answer leads us to trying to prove our point in a conversation. This, in effect, pushes us apart, and closes us down to differing perspectives and ideas. Nobody is ever totally right—or totally wrong, for that matter.

Learning to listen for what connects us is a first step in creating more positive, creative conversations. Welcoming different views is like tuning in to each other. Think how often you hear someone ask, "Are we on the same wavelength here?" To get there, you can adjust the dial on more of your senses—like Evelyn Glennie and Gary Diggins teach us to—in order to really tune in to each other.

Ask yourself regularly: How are we more alike than different? It takes real human-level listening. What might you discover?

How, where, when, with whom, might you apply this habit in your work and life?

Practice this habit for one full day. What do you notice and learn?

After one week of using this habit in your life and work, what is different?

Return to this habit after one month. How has it impacted you, your conversations, your relationships, your leadership, your work, and your life? How do you now rate yourself as a listener?

HABIT 10
CARE ABOUT WHAT'S IMPORTANT

Your mind works faster than your mouth. When someone else is speaking, it's natural for your mind to race ahead, analyse, and make your own interpretation of what you're hearing. When this is so, can you really catch what the other person cares about, or listen below the noise to hear what's important? Are you listening to your own thoughts, or truly to the other person's words?

I practiced this today as I listened to Simon and Garfunkel's "The Sound of Silence" on the radio. I wanted to have an immersive moment with a song that defines my teenage years. I turned up the radio, closed my eyes, and tried to lose myself in the music. Could I hear it vibrating through my body? I almost managed to. However, I was aware of my own thoughts getting in the way.

It's almost impossible to shut our thoughts off, and stop their interference. When you can't shut them off totally, this habit calls for you to recognise where your listening attention has gone. Are you listening inside yourself? Can you close that final distance, or at least shorten it, in order to fully take in what the other person cares about? Can you hear what is most important to them?

It takes practice. Once it's a habit, you'll discover the pure joy of the music in someone else's life—and they'll be ready to listen to what you care about too.

How, where, when, with whom, might you apply this habit in your work and life?

Practice this habit for one full day. What do you notice and learn?

After one week of using this habit in your life and work, what is different?

Return to this habit after one month. How has it impacted you, your conversations, your relationships, your leadership, your work, and your life? How do you now rate yourself as a listener?

HABIT 11

BE CURIOUS TO HEAR WHAT YOU DON'T KNOW

The first 10 habits build on one another. Can you hear their rhythm? The more you practice listening in order to connect and hear what others care about, the more you learn about them.

One habit that's evolved during the 2020 lockdown is our casual greeting, "How are you?" We have become more curious, and now ask a deeper version of the question: "How are you *really* today?" Try it with the next person you meet. Watch for a slightly longer pause, and a more considered reply.

When someone asks how you are, pause for a breath, then really listen inside yourself. *How am I really today?* Practice putting more detail into your answer. In Scotland, we're really bad at this. When someone asks how we are, we tend to say "not bad," which is an understated Scottish way of saying "I'm good." We dare not let ourselves or others know how good we really are, which makes me laugh. How will I ever know more about you if I only ask a superficial question, and receive a surface-level answer? I'm curious to learn what I don't already know about your day, work, family, interests, and life.

In workshops, we often invite participants to share something that others don't already know about them. It's amazing, especially when we do this among team members who have worked together for some time. They always discover there's more to hear in each other than they had assumed. "I thought I knew you," they'll say. "Now I realise I've never really listened fully to learn more about you." What new insights might you learn about each other today?

How, where, when, with whom, might you apply this habit in your work and life?

Practice this habit for one full day. What do you notice and learn?

After one week of using this habit in your life and work, what is different?

Return to this habit after one month. How has it impacted you, your conversations, your relationships, your leadership, your work, and your life? How do you now rate yourself as a listener?

HABIT 12
S.T.O.P. TALKING (SO THE OTHER PERSON CAN TALK)

A client shared that his boss never listens to him. Whenever my client needs to ask her something, she buzzes around her office, tidies her desk, checks her phone, or preps for her next meeting. My advice is to stop speaking, and see if his boss acknowledges the silence. (I do this with my husband when I realise he's not paying attention. Eventually, he recognises that I need him to listen.)

Here's a more direct option: *ask* the other person to listen. Why don't we do that as a habit—actually ask the other person, "Do you have time to listen to me for a second?" That would be a great and respectful way to create a true listening space, and help the other person focus in.

Here's a quote from an early client, which continues to be a personal favourite: "Listening IS respect in action." There's no greater way to show respect for each other than to stop talking, and take time to listen.

The habit here is:

- **S**top and pay attention.
- **T**ell yourself everything else can wait.
- **O**pen your ears rather than your mouth.
- **P**ay full attention to each other.

Stopping means that you also stop talking *over* one another. If we all talked over each other, the world would be a constant drone of noise. Nothing useful would be said or heard. Remember, the words *silent* and *listen* are composed of the same letters. It takes being silent to truly listen.

How, where, when, with whom, might you apply this habit in your work and life?

Practice this habit for one full day. What do you notice and learn?

After one week of using this habit in your life and work, what is different?

Return to this habit after one month. How has it impacted you, your conversations, your relationships, your leadership, your work, and your life? How do you now rate yourself as a listener?

HABIT 13
AGREEMENT AND COMPLETION

There's a powerful scene in the movie *Jerry Maguire*, when Renée Zellweger's character tells Tom Cruise's character, "You complete me." Okay, maybe you're not as into this *chick flick moment* as I am. Still, there's something inspiring if you are willing to hear it.

Much of our listening is incomplete. We move on before agreeing that the conversation is complete, without confirming exactly what we've heard, or what's been shared. A common question at the end of a coaching conversation is to ask, "Are we complete?" This process-related question is intended to check if there's anything left unsaid, and to be sure that the conversation has reached a satisfactory conclusion.

A great habit to use at the end of any conversation is to ask completion-mined questions:

"Are we complete?"

"Do you have what you need?"

"Is there anything left unsaid?"

"Are we clear on what we'll each do next?"

Taking a few extra seconds to ask completion-minded questions can save time in the long run. They help ensure that everyone has heard the same outcome, and are confident and trusting that you can go off and take next steps. This habit can take your trust in conversations and their outcomes to new levels.

How, where, when, with whom, might you apply this habit in your work and life?

Practice this habit for one full day. What do you notice and learn?

After one week of using this habit in your life and work, what is different?

Return to this habit after one month. How has it impacted you, your conversations, your relationships, your leadership, your work, and your life? How do you now rate yourself as a listener?

HABIT 14
ENJOY THE SILENCE

There's no need to be afraid of, or uncomfortable in silence. In fact, it's natural to be uncomfortable in silent space, especially in a world where we are taught that we must always be *on*.

The fact is, silence is a gift. Give it at the start of every meeting and conversation. Create a moment for everyone, including yourself, to pause and be silent before jumping into the agenda. Create silent moments between meetings as well. I suggest to all my clients that they create 10-minute 'silences' between meetings, so they have space to process each conversation, and prepare for the next.

You can also allow silence to stretch for longer intervals after you ask a question. Doing so gives the other person time to think about an answer. Our brains need silence to process what we're hearing. Learn to love and listen to the silence. When you feel the urge to start speaking again, practice staying quiet just a little longer. I can almost guarantee the other person will say something interesting.

Remember from the previous habit that the words *silent* and *listen* have the same letters. Silence invites a deeper form of listening. What do you hear in each other when you say nothing at all?

How, where, when, with whom, might you apply this habit in your work and life?

Practice this habit for one full day. What do you notice and learn?

After one week of using this habit in your life and work, what is different?

Return to this habit after one month. How has it impacted you, your conversations, your relationships, your leadership, your work, and your life? How do you now rate yourself as a listener?

LISTEN POEM

When I ask you to listen to me and you start giving advice, you
have not done what I asked.
When I ask you to listen to me
and you begin to tell me why I shouldn't feel that way, you are
trampling on my feelings.
When I ask you to listen to me
and you feel you have to do something to solve my problem,
you have failed me, strange as that may seem.
Listen! All I asked was that you listen.
Not talk or do—just hear me.
When you do something for me that I can and need to do for
myself, you contribute to my fear and weakness.
But when you accept as a simple fact that I do feel what I feel,
no matter how irrational,
then I can quit trying to convince you
and can get about the business of understanding
what's behind this irrational feeling.

And when that's clear, the answers are obvious and I don't need advice.

Irrational feelings make sense when we understand what's behind them.

So please listen and just hear me.

And if you want to talk, wait a minute for your turn;

Then I'll listen to you.

–Anonymous, *generally thought to have come from the world of counselling.*

SECTION THREE

LISTENING TO THE WORLD

"The earth has music for those who listen." [12]

—George Santayana

MY STORY

Part Three

For eight days in August, 2019, I lived in a very different world. My normal world disappeared, along with all of the noise it usually contained. The hospital's environment—bustling, caring, ever-moving, personal yet impersonal—became my world.

Arriving there on the evening before surgery, I almost felt like I was going on holiday. I had packed my bag with everything I'd need for an anticipated week-long stay. I was assigned to my bed on Ward 205—the neuro surgery ward of Aberdeen's Foresterhill Hospital. I spent a leisurely evening in the TV room with friends, watching a soap opera, and flicking through a magazine.

I felt relaxed and curious. I watched and listened to every small detail as the nursing staff took my vitals and made notes on my chart. Mr. Kamel came by briefly to confirm he'd meet me outside the operating room at 9 a.m.

I slept well.

I didn't get much time to talk with my husband when he came in early the next morning, as a procession of specialists came by to prepare me for surgery.

A cheery orderly named Jim came to wheel me toward the operating room.

"Let's get this party started," he said.
"Did you bring the prosecco?" I asked.

My husband waved me off into the lift, entrusting me to Jim's careful driving as we made our way through the twists and turns of the hospital's corridors. He'd traversed these halls for more than 20 years, and knew what to listen for in pre-op patients as we chatted cheerily along the way.

He handed me over to the theatre team. They slid me onto a sheepskin blanket, and my anaesthetists approached with an oxygen mask. I guess it wasn't just oxygen. I woke nine and a half hours later, in the exact same spot, looking at the same clock, at the same faces, and hearing myself completing the same conversation I'd started all those hours earlier.

It was bizarre and other-worldly.

"That didn't take so long then," I commented on seeing the clock face read 6:30 p.m., which was three hours earlier than they'd predicted. I felt like I'd gotten off easy. Until, that is, I spent the next 18 nauseous hours in the ICU as my body reacted to the aftermath of the anaesthetic.

ICU nurses and doctors are incredible. A dedicated nurse asked me questions every 30 minutes to check my responses and alertness. Meanwhile, they kept me pumped full of steroids and antibiotics to ward off any swelling and potential infections.

During those hours, I learned to listen to my own sense of time. Looking at the clock meant nothing. Watching clock hands circle slowly was adding to the pain. Instead, I listened in a micro-meditative way. Each moment was a pinpoint, but also a vast depth of time. It was the only space in which I existed. I listened into it and realised that I could hear only my own sense of being. Everything else was outside of me.

For a night, this was my whole world.

I carried this feeling through the following days. I was moved from ICU to a close-observation ward for three nights, then back to the normal ward for another four days.

Before heading into the hospital, I had prepared a package for my husband to bring to me. I thought I'd need several books, a journal and a pen, and of course my phone to get me through the long days. Each day he brought the package in, and asked if I wanted it. Each day I declined. Even by day four I had no need to listen to anything outside of the world in which I currently existed.

I preferred to stay curious, to listen and engage with everything going on around me, to question the nurses and doctors who tended to me. Curious about how my treatment was being pre-scribed, I listened with eyes and ears to how the ward operated.

Time passed beautifully—one long, meditative experience of just being present to each moment, and each next step of the procedure, interspersed with visits from friends and family.

It was a strange and peaceful new world into which I listened.

LISTENING TO THE WORLD

"Deep listening involves listening to the other while also listening to what is emerging from yourself. It goes beyond the words, and requires attunement to the space around us, not only the words being spoken." [13]

Eight months after my surgery, this quote, via the Facebook page of Otto Scharmer's Presencing Institute, brought me to reflect on my hospital world.

For eight days, I was a part of that world—not a victim in it. Nobody was making my experience *happen* to me. My listening made me part of it, and shaped how I experienced every person and activity I encountered.

It changed how I listen in my everyday world. Even now, I still take more time to listen to myself, and to others. I hear more when I'm not living at speed. I'm more and more curious about our world, and how it's changing amidst the upheaval of the

2020 pandemic: a year of social and economic disruption that we didn't hear coming.

What does it mean to listen to the world?

In one sense, my hospital world was specific, narrow, and temporary. In another sense, by stripping away all of my usual daily experiences, and opening up to something I'd never undergone before, the hospital world was a deeply, all-encompassing, potentially dangerous, and somewhat scary place.

However, I didn't *hear* it like that. The way I chose to *listen* to that world turned it into the experience that it was. My listening was the key to how I navigated it.

Months later, finding myself in Canada as the lockdown started, I again chose listening as my response to a new and unknown world.

I listened to my own emotions through uncertainty; fearful wonder as I fell sick; impatience and anger as our flights were cancelled; gratitude that I didn't face any real hardship; and eventually patience as we sat through the lockdown, watching the world from our window.

I listened to my doctors until we found a solution to my intermittent cough. I listened to my clients as their emotions took them on roller coasters of highs and lows. I listened to my coaching peers as they rushed to help and rescue, even before it was clear what people needed. I listened to my friends as we created Zoom calls and online family quizzes to connect with each other.

And, I listened to the cascade of online meetings, videos, training course, talks, advisors, and news feeds until it became so noisy I couldn't take any more. Had this really become our world? What were we hearing in this new unknown? What were we listening for?

Amidst everything, a phrase that had come out of a conversation with my then apprentice, Cathy, kept squeezing its way into my mind.

"Stay curious," it said.

"Be radically curious," it pleaded.

"Get more and more curious," it urged.

Listen, listen, listen. And learn.

So I did. I listened. And I learned that most of what we hear are our own thoughts and feelings. What we hear becomes our experience, and shapes our words, actions and responses. What we hear is what we make real.

I learned that to listen fully means to hear the questions under the surface—those not being asked, and possibilities not yet heard.

I learned that choosing different words—even small ones—can create big shifts in how we experience the world. For me, "back to normal," became "a new normal," which soon transitioned into "a new better."

I recalled that on just about any leadership retreat I'd been on for years, sitting in a circle, perhaps sharing poetry, listening to each other more attentively than usual, someone had, at some point, started a sentence with, "Back in the real world..." Here's the thing: there is no *back*. The world we experience now, every day, is the real one.

Isn't it?

One day, during a break from writing, I went for a short walk around the woodland and river trail by my house. I was almost home, strolling under a canopy of ancient trees, the sun glinting through the over-hanging branches, when I 'heard' a strong urging behind me. I didn't look round, but I'm pretty sure there was no one following me.

I heard and felt generations of ancestors urging me forward. My mind imagined beautiful faces and hands gently pushing me on. In front of me sang what sounded like the clamour of young, vibrant, enthusiastic voices. I imagined they belonged to the next generation of listeners, eager to be heard.

I stopped for a moment to just listen.

There was a time when I wouldn't have 'heard' such a moment, far less confess to it in writing. As I get older though, I'm less concerned with what you hear when I write about that moment. Instead, I'm more curious about such a moment, and what it seeks to teach me.

A moment of 'silence' in nature is never totally quiet. The natural world is always talking to us, and supporting our human journey. Whilst I'm not an expert in that field, I've had other moments like the one above, when I've listened to nature.

I heard it once on a 'forest bathing' experience in the Rocky Mountains, with my friend Ronna Schneberger. Ronna takes busy executives out into the forest to bring quiet to their stressed minds and bodies. Science has proven that such experiences have physical and psychological benefits.

To quote Ronna:

- 15 minutes in nature will reduce your cortisol (stress hormone) levels by 12%

- 2 hours in nature will increase your memory and attention span by 20%
- 3 days in nature will increase your cancer-fighting blood cells by 56%

When you're in nature with Ronna, you discover just how much there is to really listen to. You can literally hear the trees breathing.

One of the beautiful things about the 2020 lockdown is how it forced many people outdoors for exercise, where we walked or cycled in nature, rather than in air-conditioned gyms.

My house is hidden away in a quiet corner, yet only minutes from town. During lockdown, roughly 40 people a day came upon its peaceful beauty as they walked the normally deserted woodland trail nearby. Let's hope those walkers listened more fully to the subtle sounds of nature, and that they've carried these new sounds with them as the post-lockdown world opens again.

Whether we add an extra 10 seconds of listening to each other, or 15 minutes listening in nature, there's no doubt that the world is calling us to listen more deeply. And, it comes full circle.

Listening to the world means listening to ourselves more deeply as well. I know you've already 'heard' me mention this twice, but it bears repeating one last time: the words *listen* and *silent* have the same letters. Listening creates silence. Silence invites listening. We can listen with our breath to the rhythms of the earth, rather than to the speed of our cellphones.

Our crazy, changing world consumes our energy, and divides our attention. We hear complaints and conflict, but miss moments of connection and caring. We worry about the needs of others, but struggle to acknowledge our own. Problems rattle our ears, but possibilities go unheard. We listen attentively to our heads, but must fight to hear what's in our hearts.

Since COVID-19, our known ways have been disrupted, sending echoes into many layers of life, and turning up the volume on issues we've been deaf to for some time.

Isn't it revealing how we've neglected to question the darker side of many political, educational, financial and regulatory institutions for so long?

Sadly, one of the easiest, most comfortable paths to walk is to accept what we're told by teachers, parents, bosses, TV, the press—you name it—and not question what we hear.

As disruption continues to unfold, it's hard not to wonder what kind of world we will create through better listening.

HABITS 15 – 21

LISTENING TO THE WORLD

15. Listen for New Perspectives

16. Listen with Head, Heart and Hand

17. We ARE All Connected

18. Practice Radical Curiosity

19. Blue Sky Listening

20. Leave a Legacy of Listening

21. Create Listening Circles

HABIT 15
LISTEN FOR NEW PERSPECTIVES

Set the intention to listen for new perspectives in the world each day. You might listen with a fully open mind to someone you don't know, or have just met. Or, you might read a newspaper or a book on a topic you don't normally read. You may even listen to some music that's unfamiliar to you, or ask a question that starts a conversation on a topic you're hesitant to dig into.

Perhaps you'll ask a question that feels a bit scary.

Notice what you hear when your world expands in new directions. Listen for what you've been missing.

How, where, when, with whom, might you apply this habit in your work and life?

Practice this habit for one full day. What do you notice and learn?

After one week of using this habit in your life and work, what is different?

Return to this habit after one month. How has it impacted you, your conversations, your relationships, your leadership, your work, and your life? How do you now rate yourself as a listener?

HABIT 16

LISTEN WITH HEAD, HEART AND HAND

I've listened to plenty of podcasts and webinars during the 2020 lockdown, when many of the world's biggest thinkers have been exploring what this time of change could mean. In one thought-provoking broadcast between Otto Scharmer, Frederick Laloux and Amy Fox, I heard how important it is for us to listen in new ways to uncover deeper possibilities for real transformation.[14]

During their conversation, they suggested that we're all pretty good at listening with our heads, and applying our intellectual capacity as we think about what could change.

The next layer of listening happens when we start to feel something more deeply—in our heart. This triggers our emotions, and brings new issues into our awareness. Something literally stirs inside us, and sends our blood pumping.

This aligns with how Evelyn Glennie and Gary Diggins demonstrate ways we can expand our capacity for listening by using our bodies, and all of our senses.

However, it isn't until we move to the *third* level that real change happens. What is the third level? Our hands. This is the level of action. Our world is calling us into action right now. Where are *you* being called into action?

How, where, when, with whom, might you apply this habit in your work and life?

Practice this habit for one full day. What do you notice and learn?

After one week of using this habit in your life and work, what is different?

Return to this habit after one month. How has it impacted you, your conversations, your relationships, your leadership, your work, and your life? How do you now rate yourself as a listener?

HABIT 17

WE ARE ALL CONNECTED

It's taken me a long time to even get close to the meaning behind the idea that we are all connected. I have to go beyond just hearing the words intellectually.

Deep listening seems to be the gateway to fully appreciate what it means when we say we are all connected. Science tells us there is a brain intelligence in our hearts and guts, as well as in our heads. Plus, we're all made of the same cellular material. In fact, Brian Cox, a British physicist, describes how we are all made from the same cellular molecules that formed our planet.[15]

In that way, we are all truly connected across millions of years of evolution. It's mind-boggling. We are literally made of the same material as the very planet on which we stand, sit, walk, sleep, breathe…and on which we listen.

This awareness invites us to listen more deeply in so many ways—and makes listening an even more fascinating process to explore. When you listen from the part of you that knows *we are all connected* at cellular and celestial levels, you come to realise that listening to others is like listening to parts of yourself. Therefore, listening to yourself more fully is like listening to what you can bring out in others.

It's a deeper, healthier, and more mysterious way to hear our world. Make it a habit to listen for the mysteries of connection everywhere around you.

How, where, when, with whom, might you apply this habit in your work and life?

Practice this habit for one full day. What do you notice and learn?

After one week of using this habit in your life and work, what is different?

Return to this habit after one month. How has it impacted you, your conversations, your relationships, your leadership, your work, and your life? How do you now rate yourself as a listener?

HABIT 18
PRACTICE RADICAL CURIOSITY

As humans, curiosity is our natural state of being. We witness this in children, hearing it in their wonder and their cries. However, as adults, we complain or grow impatient with their incessant questions. Meanwhile, our modern institutions don't create space to live fully in the world of curiosity. Exams herd us toward *right* answers, while jobs coral us into stagnation, and silence curiosity with steady doses of *this is how we do things around here* thinking.

Returning to a world of curiosity invites you to ask new questions, and pay attention to where the questions take you. In the current world, many questions point back to the past, from where we analyse and work out what's gone wrong, and measure progress against what's always been. In his book, *A More Beautiful Question*, Warren Berger suggests a process of question-storming as a way to open our minds, and get more curious about the future.[16] It involves asking, asking, and asking some more, until you discover breakthrough insights and ideas. In Berger's experience, groups generate roughly 40 questions before new ideas emerge.

It takes a true investment in time, effort and curiosity to stay with questions for that long. If that's where the real curiosity pays off, it invites you to slow down and follow a process of listening, asking...listening, asking...listening, asking...on and on. To do so, and to hear something new, you have to let go of what you already know. How might you introduce the practice of radical curiosity to hear more in—and beyond—your world?

How, where, when, with whom, might you apply this habit in your work and life?

Practice this habit for one full day. What do you notice and learn?

After one week of using this habit in your life and work, what is different?

Return to this habit after one month. How has it impacted you, your conversations, your relationships, your leadership, your work, and your life? How do you now rate yourself as a listener?

HABIT 19
BLUE SKY LISTENING

The world can be a foggy, messy place. It's no wonder we listen for what we already know—we appreciate the guideposts as we go along. As the previous habit mentions, to create a new world, we must listen to what we don't yet know.

To go further with this thought, we must do so receptively. In that way, the listening space expands and increases when you have the courage to say "I don't know," and open up to what's being clouded by your judgements and assumptions.

We're fascinated by the beauty of a bright blue sky, and can feel its expanse so full of mystery and possibility. It seems endless and infinite. What if our hearing can take us similarly beyond the messy noise of the day, and open up huge, infinite spaces where there's always something else to hear?

What do you hear when you admit that you don't know the answer? Do you feel clearer in a funny kind of way? We assume clarity means getting to a clear answer. What if clarity actually means letting go of all the noise, and finding the one clear note that hasn't been heard?

Dare to listen IN to the space in front of you—the future you don't yet know.

How, where, when, with whom, might you apply this habit in your work and life?

Practice this habit for one full day. What do you notice and learn?

After one week of using this habit in your life and work, what is different?

Return to this habit after one month. How has it impacted you, your conversations, your relationships, your leadership, your work, and your life? How do you now rate yourself as a listener?

HABIT 20
LEAVE A LEGACY OF LISTENING

In a recent *Forbes* article, neuroscientist David Rock suggests that listening deeply is the first step in making sure people feel heard in these times of disruption and change.[17] It's one of the few things that can calm deeply emotional situations.

He quotes what FBI negotiators do, like other crisis professionals, in hostage and conflict situations. "They listen so well that people feel heard more than they ever have," he writes.

What if your legacy as a leader were to be one of listening—of leaving a world where people felt you truly listened, and fully heard them? How might you demonstrate that legacy daily with each person you meet? I'd be happy with something to that effect on my tombstone: "She really listened and heard me."

How, where, when, with whom, might you apply this habit in your work and life?

Practice this habit for one full day. What do you notice and learn?

After one week of using this habit in your life and work, what is different?

Return to this habit after one month. How has it impacted you, your conversations, your relationships, your leadership, your work, and your life? How do you now rate yourself as a listener?

HABIT 21
CREATE LISTENING CIRCLES

Bring together a group of friends, family, colleagues, or even people you don't know very well. Set a fixed duration for your listening circle—perhaps 30 minutes initially—and explain that the circle is only for people to listen and be heard.

You might pick a topic, or ask a question. Then, give everyone five minutes to speak what's on their minds or in their hearts in relation to that topic or question. Everyone receives time and space to share their thoughts and feelings, without judgement or argument.

Once everyone has spoken, sit in silence as a group for another few minutes, then ask everyone to share one word on what their experience was like. Thank everyone for their contribution, and close the circle. I also suggest that people feel free to journal or reflect on what they've heard, and to listen deeply to how it affects or shifts their perspectives, moods, or feelings about themselves or the world.

Insights and learning will come in waves—even after the listening circle has ended. What if, at least once a week, your business meeting took the form of a listening circle? What would you and others hear?

How, where, when, with whom, might you apply this habit in your work and life?

Practice this habit for one full day. What do you notice and learn?

After one week of using this habit in your life and work, what is different?

Return to this habit after one month. How has it impacted you, your conversations, your relationships, your leadership, your work, and your life? How do you now rate yourself as a listener?

IT'S TIME

It's time for the light

to enfold and embrace

the thoughts and the fear and

the branches of darkness

that stretch through our lives

all twisted and curled

protected by moss,

wet, yet brittle,

speckled with choices of possible paths;

encouraged by the warmth

of a white sun

whose light reaches our hearts

through fog and mist

tickling us

with diamond droplets: the dews of our future.

–Aileen Gibb, 2006

CLOSING

"Listening often means looking for what's possible."

–*Kay Lindhal,* The Sacred Art of Listening

Did you notice what happened the first time you saw the cover of this book? Take another look at it. Does your ear tip towards your left shoulder—just as it might when you cock your ears to listen to someone? I love how my designer, Lieve, captured this subtle listening movement, and translated it into a cover design. I mention it now to emphasise how subtle the body's listening response can be, until we notice it fully.

Does the large L of the cover remind you of anything else?

It occurred to me, after we'd landed on this design, that it is very similar to the 'L' plate shown on the rear windscreen when a learner driver is in the car. It invites us all to remember we're still learning to listen.

I still consider myself a learning listener. Yes, there are times when I bring my well-honed skill to the fore. Likewise, there are other times when I get too casual with things. My listening goes on autopilot, just like those times when I drive to a destination, arrive, and wonder how I got there.

I wrote this book as an exploration of what I am still learning in the lifelong experiment of listening. I'm not sure I'll ever fully 'pass the test' and be awarded my full license. The joy and adventure lie in the continual exploration and curiosity of the world and people around me.

Listening is a never-ending practice, and I'm grateful that my work keeps me in the midst of it daily, weekly, monthly, and year after year. There's always more waiting to be heard.

I listened and learned as the pages of this book unfolded.

I learned that one of *Harvard Business Review's* most downloaded articles is one on listening from 1957, making it as old as me.

I learned there's an International Association for Listening. There's also an *International Listening Journal* (www.listen.org), which was founded in 1979 (the year I got married, though I'm sure that's a coincidence). The journal's impressive library of research articles and listening case studies cuts across many sectors, including health, education, sports, business and spirituality. Think of almost any sector of our world, and someone has looked at it through the lens of listening.

I came across many questionnaires to self-assess listening skills. One of the earliest is the "Brown-Carlsen Listening Comprehension Test" from 1955— even older than I am!

I found numerous articles on listening in all the main business publications: more than 10 in *Harvard Business Review*, 20 in *Forbes*, 15 in *Fast Company*, 20 in *Entrepreneur*. And, if you type the word "listening" into the search box on TED.com, you'll call up 916 talks! Plus, an ever-increasing number of podcasts give you a chance to listen and learn even more about listening.

Search Google for "listening training," and you'll find 450 million hits!

Almost every aspect of how we behave and interact as human beings involves a form of listening. I came across list after list describing many variations of listening, everything from Appreciative Listening to Dialogic Listening, Selective Listening to Therapeutic Listening, Empathic, Relationship, Mindful...a veritable A-to-Z of listening.

Listening remains a constant feature in our human journey. We have been exploring, or at least trying to work out how to listen better, for much longer than the six decades of my lifetime. In fact, wise words on listening are attributed to philosophers as far back as Lao Tzu and Rumi.

So, how can it be that, despite all of this wisdom, effort and attention, we're still not listening well? The world is designed to get in the way. Why do we continue to listen to the superficial noise that consumes our energy, when we could have the gift of listening deeply, and thereby learning, gaining insight, and appreciating ourselves and our world more fully?

It wasn't until I heard an episode of Oscar Trimboli's *Deep Listening* podcast, that I began to give conscious thought as to why, as children, we're not trained to listen better.[18]

After all, we're taught to read, write, and speak—but not to listen. Well, okay...perhaps as children, we're told to "sit down and listen," but it's taken for granted that we know how to do so. Similarly, we're not taught how to be listened to, or fully heard.

Yes, most of us are born with the equipment we need to listen, and it is something we do automatically. However, without conscious attention, listening has become a neglected, and under-utilised skill.

For nine and a half hours in August of 2019, my listening was completely shut off. Those hours can never be reclaimed, and will remain a mystery forever. Can it be a coincidence that I, whose work in the world largely centres around listening, would have a scary, yet totally benign, tumour growing on my acoustic nerve—the very tool we use to listen?

I named my tumour Shona. She was a 41mm-long vestibular schwannoma. Also known as an acoustic neuroma, it is a silent condition that grows sneakily inside the head. Shona might have been growing on my acoustic nerve for a good part of my life—perhaps since my 20s. The image of my brainstem being pushed inwards by this golf ball-sized intruder is imprinted in my memory. Weeks, months, and now a year after Shona was evicted by the unfathomable skill of my surgeon, I continue to learn to listen to what she wanted me to hear.

She's helped me write this book, and to share more of my own story than I've done in any of my previous books.

She's helped me slow down and listen to my body and my health with new attention and focus.

She's helped me spend more time appreciating small things in nature.

She's helped me listen to my family, friends, clients, and even strangers, with greater curiosity.

She's strengthened the importance of listening in my world, and to the wider disruption that's unfolding in the world around me. In that way, she's helped to invite questions and conversations that take me into uncharted territories on what it means to live through these times.

I hope you don't have to undergo a major surgery before you learn to unlock the power of listening in your life and work. I hope that this book—and the habits I share in it—will do some of that for you.

These habits might reveal how listening can become your superpower. If it does, I hope you realise that listening is not a new superpower. It's been with us all along.

Now—right now—is a time for listening. Listening professions are on the rise. Coaching, mediating, restorative justice and many others are growing roles that bring listening to the fore. Hal Swindall, PhD, writes on the Global Listening Centre blog that, in Europe, a one-decibel rise in noise increases local assault rates by 2.6%; however, a one-decibel reduction in noise would significantly prevent 18,000 assaults per year.[19]

The power of silence, and what we hear in it, cannot be under-estimated.

Listen now: as much of the life we have come to take for granted is disrupted.

Listen now: as many of the structures we thought would always hold true start to break down and fail us.

Listen now: to the parts of life that want us to go 'back to normal'.

Listen now: as a new future opens up and invites us to step boldly toward it.

To what future are we being called? I'm curious what we'll hear.

Are you ready to *Now Listen?*

"I really need to take a time which I dedicate to create a window of listening.

I can listen to what happens in my body.

I can listen to what is in my emotional world.

I can witness my thoughts.

And I can listen to what is happening around me.

And the beauty is that meditation is a very simple process of just sitting, walking and listening.

And the listening trains our nervous system to expand an inner sense of spaciousness.

Listening creates a coherence.

And meditative states are different levels of coherence of our nervous system. Coherence creates the feeling of connectedness.

Suddenly I feel connected with life." [20]

–Thomas Hübl

REFERENCES AND RESOURCES

The act of listening is steeped in discovery, and vice versa. I'm extremely grateful for the wonderful work I've read, heard, listened to and discovered over the course of my journey, including the books, articles, podcasts and conversations that informed *Now Listen*:

1. Page 21: Shared here from: *https://www.globallisteningcentre. org/definition-of-listening/*
2. Page 26: *Volume Control: Hearing in a Deafening World*, by David Owen, by Penguin Random House, 2019.
3. Page 38: You can enjoy Evelyn Glennie's wonderful TED Talk from 2003 here: *https://www.ted.com/talks/evelyn_glennie_how_ to_truly_listen?language=en*
4. Page 42: *Beauty: The Invisible Embrace*, John O'Donohue, Harper Collins, 2004.

5. Page 42: *Seven Thousand Ways to Listen*, Mark Nepo, Simon & Shuster, 2012.

6. Page 52: You can read a transcript of Bernard Looney's 2020 "Ambition Launch, London" speech here: *https://www.bp.com/ en/global/corporate/news-and-insights/speeches/reimagining-en- ergy-reinventing-bp.html*

7. Page 57: Discover more about Marshall Goldsmith's work online at *https://www.marshallgoldsmith.com*, and access his article "Try Feed Forward Instead of Feedback" article here: *https://www.marshallgoldsmith.com/articles/try-feedforward-in- stead-feedback/*

8. Page 63: *Invocations: Poems for the Air and Ear*, Gary Diggins, independently published. You can read Gary's work online at *https://www.garydiggins.com/writings.html*

9. Page 70: There are a number of articles that point out how doctors listen, on average, for 11 seconds before they in- terrupt patients, including "11 Seconds: How Long Your Doctor Listens Before Interrupting You," by Bruce Y. Lee, published in *Forbes* online at: *https://www.forbes.com/sites/bru- celee/2018/07/22/how-long-you-can-talk-before-your-doctor-inter- rupts-you/524685cf1443*

10. Page 76: "How Real Leaders Melt the Iceberg of Ignorance with Humility," by Joost Minnaar, online at: https://corporate-rebels.com/iceberg-of-ignorance/

11. Page 77: See Margaret Heffernan's 2013 TED Talk, "The Dangers of Willful Blindness," here: *https://www.youtube.com/watch?v=Kn5JRgz3W0o*

12. Page 105: While I've attributed this quote to George Santayana, I'd like to note that this phrase has been attributed to others over time, including William Shakespeare.

13. Page 111: You can access the entire Facebook post from the Presenting Institute, dated April 22, 2020, here: *https://www.facebook.com/presencinginstitute/posts/10158208754584894*

14. Page 124: This lovely conversation took place as part of "Coaches Rising: The Future of Leadership," July, 2020: *https://courses.coachesrising.com/session/the-future-of-leadership/*

15. Page 127: Brian Cox, from "Wonders of the Universe, Episode: Stardust," BBC TWO: *https://www.bbc.co.uk/programmes/b00zm833*

16. Page 131: *A More Beautiful Question: The Power of Inquiry to Spark Breakthrough Ideas*, Warren Berger, Bloomsbury USA, 2014.

17. Page 136: "How to Be an Ally in this Moment: Listen Deeply, Unite Widely, Act Boldly," by David Rock, published in *Forbes*

online at: *https://www.forbes.com/sites/davidrock/2020/06/03/ leadership-in-this-moment-listen-deeply-unite-widely-act-bold- ly/58055bc622cd*

18. Page 148: You can listen to Oscar Trimboli's "Deep Listening" podcast here: *https://www.oscartrimboli.com/podcasts/*

19. Page 150: Read "Peaceful Silence: Noise, Aggression, and Constructive Listening," by Hal Swindall, PhD, here: *https:// www.globallisteningcentre.org/peaceful-silence-noise-aggres- sion-and-constructive-listening/*

20. Page 152: You can access Thomas Hübl's post, "Meditation is a Window of Listening," dated July 14, 2020, here: *https://www. facebook.com/Thomas.Huebl.Sangha/posts/3427762037234155*

ADDITIONAL REFERENCES AND RESOURCES

- Two people in every 100,000 are affected by acoustic neuroma (vestibular schwannoma) each year in the UK. This type of tumour is usually slow-growing. Early indicators include one-sided deafness and tinnitus, episodes of vertigo, headaches, loss of balance and dizziness, or indications of facial paralysis. In my case, I had a mysterious slight numbness along the left side of my mouth for over five years which was not identified as potential acoustic neuroma. Learn more at www.BANA-uk.com.
- *Tuning the Eardrums: Listening as a Mindful Practice,* by Gary Diggins, Friesen Press, 2016.
- My previous books: *Asking Great Questions* and *The Conversation Edge*, available on my author's page on Amazon.com.

- Evelyn Glennie's wonderful work can be fully appreciated on her website, *https://www.evelyn.co.uk*
- Kay Kay, one of my first mentors, has two lovely self-published books: *SMART LISTENING* and *SMART TALKING*. Available on Kay Kay's author's page on Amazon.com.

APPRECIATIONS

Above all, my appreciation is for the many clients, colleagues and team members I've been honoured to listen to for many years. Without the privilege of your conversations, I would not be the listener I am today. I hope the echoes of our conversations continue to inspire your deep listening.

Whenever I am asked to name the best listener I know, Gary Diggins pops to the top of the list. Those of you who know Gary will know what I mean. Gary is a role model of calm, and well-practised in the art of deep listening. Gary's approach as a teacher of listening, through the use of percussion and sound therapy, is a delight to experience. I am deeply grateful for all the listening events we've co-facilitated and created over the years.

I must also thank Kay Kay, whose words kept popping into my head as I wrote this book. Indeed, I originally wanted to steal the title of an article we co-wrote many years ago, and call this book *Listen for a Change*. The threads of that original concept weave their way throughout *Now Listen*, and I am grateful for the listening I received from Kay Kay in the earlier phases of my work.

I am more than grateful—and still in awe—of the amazing medical team at Ward 205, Aberdeen Royal Infirmary, in the Foresterhill site (the Foresterhill Hospital, as we call it locally).

I got to my sixth decade without any major need for medical support. Lying in my hospital bed for eight days, I was struck that everyone, from super-skilled surgeons, to devoted, yet light-hearted student nurses and ward orderlies, were doing 'real work' that makes a huge difference every day. Words truly can't express how vital and yet under-valued this work is. My gratitude defies description, and I will continue to live in full appreciation of all those who work in and volunteer time toward the caring professions.

I am grateful for family, friends, and of course, my husband Jake, for the love and support shared with me during that time as well.

And my gratitude again for the beautiful design work on this book by Lieve Maas of Bright Light Graphics. I am so glad we found each other, and for your ability to 'get' me and my ideas.

And to my editor, Dave Jarecki, for this, our second collaboration. I trust your skills to take my writing to a higher level. I appreciate all you teach me.

ABOUT THE AUTHOR

As an author, Aileen Gibb mines her decades of conversation, coaching, facilitation and leadership experience with clients around the world, turning real-life stories into invaluable, everyday tools, tips and techniques which make a difference to people in all walks of life. Conversation, she believes, is a fundamentally unique part of being human, and of being in relationship with each other. "In conversation, we meet ourselves at new edges of insight and understanding," she says. "When we discover what lies beyond those edges, everything shifts." Aileen splits her time between her Scottish homeland, and her adopted home in the Rocky Mountains of Canada. She gains inspiration from both landscapes, as well as from her conversations with mission-driven individuals and organisations, with whom she coaches. To explore Aileen's work, or to contact her for a conversation, got to www.aileengibb.com.

Manufactured by Amazon.ca
Bolton, ON

18192067R00092